GW00459121

# The Saucy Minx Poems
# Vol I

For Mother Superior, with eternal thanks.

Nov xxx

HalleLOLjah!

**Dear Reader,**

A little sauce can season the dish of life. All that follows is simply for fun and not intended to cause offence. Bear in mind, should you choose to read on, that any word is only as rude as your own imagination allows it to be, (well, more or less).

**Yours Sincerely,**

**A.N.**

The Saucy Minx Poems Vol I

**Copyright © 2023**

# Table of Contents

*Santa's coming!*

# Ode to a Euphoric Yuletide

As Christmas approaches, there's something I lack a

Strong hand to assist me with pulling my cracker …

A tug on your own is just never as good,

Help me out and I'll give you a taste of my pud.

If that doesn't tempt – are you into mulled wine?

If yule show me yours then I'll let you see mine.

I love all the baubles on your Christmas tree,

You've hung them so well, and well-hung just suits me!

Let's sweep out the hearth and make it inviting …

To see Santa coming is oh, so exciting!

Sure, it's giving, not getting that we should indulge in,

But I think I'll get plenty – see how his sack's bulging!

Now, onto the dinner – the turkey needs stuffing,

Keep pushing that sausage to help get enough in.

Do you want breast or thigh? Ooh, it all looks so great,

You just can't get too much when it's laid on a plate!

So, please raise your glass at this time of good cheer,

And don't forget – your bird's ready when her juices run clear!

******

*Vintage Garden Delights*

# Ode to a Gorgeous Gardener

Springtime has sprung and the garden is stirring,

Sweet birdsong proclaims that new life is occurring.

When I hear the whir of a distant lawn mower,

I put down my teacup and get on the blower.


Now, some like a man in a smart business suit,

While some find a uniform terribly cute,

But I don't need a man who is suited and booted,

When what I most want's to get rooted and shooted.


For I want to see fresh, green shoots when it's spring,

To know the joy this lady's garden can bring,

So, come over now and distribute your seed,

Plant tulips right here (and my rose needs a feed).


There's some overgrowth there that necessitates strimming,

So, helmet and harness – I'll help to get him in;

With my helping hand, I am ready and willing,

When so many pots in my garden want filling.

An abundance of birdies is busily nesting,

The sheen of their feathers is pretty arresting;

A huge plump woodpecker on my table sits,

And the birdbath – so bracing – see? I've got blue tits.


Mesmerised, I gaze into the pond on the lawn,

Watching frogs at their business – are they making frogs'
porn?

My tools are all yours for when you're on the go,

I just know you're the best man to handle this hoe…


What's produced by my gardener has the top taste,

I'll gobble it down, not a speck shall I waste.

You'll find nothing to match this at Lidl or Tesco;

When the sun shines, my gardener serves me al fresco.


So, tackle my trellis and fill this bird's bath,

Please lead the way, Darling, up my garden path;

For I know no other man ever will do –

When I long and I yearn to be green fingered too!


******


6

*Sturdy and erect!*

# Ode to a Beautiful Bricklayer

The architect's drawings are all good to go,

There's a rumour the plumber might actually show;

Planning officer's happy – they love a good payer –

I'm delighted it's time now to find a brick layer.


For there's little in life that can give greater kicks,

Than watching an expert at work with his bricks.

When you need an erection, there's no-one who's mastered

More, getting things up in good time to get plastered.


It takes a big trucker to carry this load,

I can feel the earth move as he drives up my road.

If he wants all the goods on site on the first day,

Let's get on the job – what's the point in delay?


With brick upon brick and row upon row,

I'm breathless just watching my brick layer go;

A real life Colossus from lugging his hod,

But far better 'entroweled' than your average Greek god.

Deft hands that work hard can soon get a bit rough,

But Swarfega is fab – I've a vat of the stuff!

So come here and bring your best brick layer's mate –

Don't all singles need tingles in their tingle plate?

You've wooed me so well, your string lines are the best,

And we'll soon put the strength of that wall to the test;

If things dry too fast, a girl can get demented,

But with you in the mix this love's truly cemented!

******

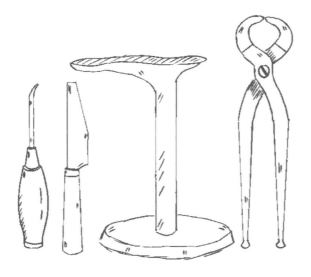

*The right tools for the job.*

# Ode to a Courtly Cobbler

Walking the pavements at times takes its toll,

Causing damage to heels and a wearing of sole,

So, when footwear trouble has made me a hobbler,

I'll make a beeline to my favourite cobbler.


He's an old-fashioned sort and his shop is quite charming,

His entrance bell tinkles, the sound is disarming,

Ah, the sweet smell of leather assails my nose,

I'll show him my job and suggest that he close …


So he'll shut up his shop to give me his attention,

I've got a 'to-do' list that's too long to mention.

Behind the oak counter his tools are all hanging –

(The neighbours are used to the buzzes and banging).


Collars, vamps, aglets, small, medium, large –

He'll see to them all for a reasonable charge;

Boots, thigh-high, heels sky-high, wedge, Cuban or kitten,

He'll zip up, not slip up, and thus am I smitten.

A foot fetish fantasy?  Give me a shout!

And gaze at these lace-ups (with tongue hanging out);

Or, I'll don my Blahniks, and you'll know your place

Is face-down on the counter, my heels on your base…


With these lush Hush Puppies you'll know loafer heaven,

Where size matters not, (if at least a size seven) …

That suits me just fine, (I don't mean to be picky),

Watch out with that glue gun – your pumps could get sticky.


The fumes from the solvents can make me feel high;

Time spent with my cobbler just seems to fly by

In this hedonist heaven of buckle and belt –

(And, between friends, what matters the odd weal or welt?)


So, fix me up, Cobbler, and, back on my feet,

In comfort once more I'll explore lane and street.

I'm a cobbler gobbler, for one who so woos me,

Some quality custom, so just (Jimmy) Choos me!


\*\*\*\*\*\*

*Safely under lock and key*

# Ode to a Luscious Locksmith

When a night out has come to its glorious end,
And I'm poured in a taxi by my bestest friend,
As the cab pulls up in my familiar street,
I get out, but don't notice my keys on the seat…

Oh My!  How did this happen?!  The third time this year!
But I know what to do, and that I needn't fear,
For, dear Locksmith, you'll come when I give you a call,
So we can gain access to my entrance hall.

I'll wait on the steps – you'll be here in a minute,
With a shiny new lock and a key to go in it.
I'll trust the method my locksmith devises,
(Hasps differ in width, but you know what my size is).

You can build up the tension with your tension tool,
(Your 'feather touch' tension wrench works as a rule),
With your formed-end tweezers, you're an expert wiggler,
Am I bad to be glad of your auto-jiggler?

So, come on now, Locksmith, get me in my hall,

As you apply torque, I'll hang on to the wall;

Get in, shoot your bolt and then with any luck,

I'll call you next time I'm in need of a … lock.

******

*As snug as a bug in my rug*

# Ode to a Caressable Carpet Fitter

This linoleum's looking a bit worse for wear,

In hallway and stairway, the carpet's threadbare.

Upstairs in the bedrooms, things look pretty dreary;

It's true – of the same old things, one becomes weary.


I know what to do and I know who to call,

For a floor-based makeover that spans wall-to-wall,

So now that's decided, and I'll spend a bit o',

Quality time with my best carpet fitter.


See my tatty old rug?  I know he's not a fan,

I'll attend to that now before I hear his van;

But for heavier prep, there's no better man I know,

For getting it up – all of that tired old lino…


He's shown me the samples of all his goods,

(We agree, a shag pile beats any hard woods);

I'll want it quite deep and, as he promptly learns,

I'll not mind if this costs me a few carpet burns!

Ah, pure wool and nylon, seagrass and jute,

I'm testing them all out – and how! – What a hoot!

Since these are all stain-proof and splash-proof, it's clear,

That no-one could guess what's gone on over here…


So come, Carpet Fitter, and bring your tool belt,

Bring kicker and gripper – and you can get felt.

For services rendered you'll be so well paid,

But make sure, just the floor, is what gets under-laid!


****

*Hey, Sweetie!*

# Ode to an Affectionate Confectioner

With all the delights of a sumptuous repast,
I love to save the best 'til last;
From dinner, though I be replete,
I'll always find room for something sweet.

My little black book lists a great connection, a
Sweet man, eye candy and expert confectioner.
Who can resist when sweet stuff is abundant?
Resisting temptation is surely redundant.

So bring to my pad your confection equipment,
Whatever you're lacking, I'll order a shipment.
I'll keep you well-stocked, with everything cakey,
You'll be up first thing, for a wakey and bakey…

For there's little much sweeter than a sweet-talking
bachelor,
Who knows how to handle a silicon spatula,
And here is my cake stand – rotating, you see,
So whilst working with one hand, your other hand's free –

To do what you need to get icing with ease,

A steady hand giving your bag a firm squeeze,

Whilst a fresh nozzle gets its due attention –

I've a bunch of attachments, too many to mention…

Your attention to detail's second to none,

Be it chocolatey fingers or icing my bun.

In times gone by, cakes were more frugally fashioned,

(Unthinkable now, to have my sugar rationed!)

So, come on, Confectioner, sprinkle those berries,

Admire the sheen on my plump, glacé cherries.

On multiple moments, you make me rejoice –

To be candid, to be candied's my ultimate choice!

\*\*\*\*\*\*

*Yo Ho Ho!*

# Ode for a Jolly Roger(ing)

With a Blue Beard baiting,

Black Pig boarding,

Long John Silver,

Treasure-hoarding,

I'll polish your yard-arm

While you swab my decks,

Drop anchor in my shallows,

Avoiding the wrecks.

With a foul-mouthed,

Pugwashesque, pirate-talking,

Land-lubber garrotting,

Parrot squawking,

Unbuckle my swash,

Land ahoy! Me first mate,

Now come fill my Pretty Polly

With pieces of eight!

******

*S.W.A.L.K.*

# Ode to an Alpha Mail Man

Forget a young techie, MSN or email fan,

I'd prefer a French letter in the hand of my mail man.

Just ding-dong my bell or

Knock twice on my knocker,

That big, red post box is a bit of a shocker!

I'll whisper the post code I'd like you to crack,

And I'll unzip your zip code to empty your sack.


Parcel Force may be flashy, but they've nothing on you,

They go only by weight, and we know that won't do.

A sloppy delivery and my present's in tatters,

A real mail man knows, it *is* size that matters.

Ooh, that's a big package – surprisingly large!

Let me open my purse up to pay the surcharge….


Your shiny post van is impressively nippy –

Just as well – up the *country* can get a bit slippy.

Your engine's loud throbbing

Makes me feel rather quivery,

So I'll get my box ready

For your Special Delivery!

\*\*\*\*\*\*

*Hmmm, fruity and creamy…*

# A Kitchen Ode to Fruitiness

Now, naughty You,

Full of surprises,

I'll knead your dough, until it rises…

Come, suck my sweetie, lick it up,

Pile my dish and fill my cup.

Clink the glass and crack the toffee,

Take a dip in my warm banoffee!

Pop your cork and burst my berry,

Dabble in my trifle (sherry).

Come on, butter my bread,

Is this tea-time porn?

I need finishing off,

With a lovely Cream Horn!

\*\*\*\*\*\*

*Wet first, then hard!*

# Ode to a Bountiful Builder

A bad DIY-er can't handle his tool,

And an odd-job bodger won't keep his cool,

So, when a job needs doing, I'll say with a grin –

"It's time to get the builder in!"

From raising my roof, down to laying my flooring,

I'll give you a peek at my architect's drawing;

(As the ink dried, I knew there could be no objection

To the length and the breadth of my proposed erection).

I expect to see helmets when men work on-site,

They can all keep their tools in my vehicle overnight…

And for finishing off, we can put out to tender –

Myself, I quite fancy a bit of rough render.

So, get out your tools for industrial drilling,

I've a rising damp patch, and a hole that needs filling!

Come on, repoint my stonework and fix up my shutters,

Screw in my downpipe and clear out my gutters.

Be sure of your scaffold – you don't want to fall –

Come with me to test out that load-bearing wall…

If your wood's running low, then it's me you can thank-

It's a pleasure to give a good builder a

Plank!

*Fifteen ways with a 9" …*

# Ode to a Delectable Decorator

I feel the need to renew, as I glance at my ceiling,
These colours won't do, and my paintwork is peeling.
It's time, when my pad gets in this kind of state t'
Get straight on the blower to my top decorator.

Ah, he comes straight away in his clean bib and braces,
But a dab of white spirit should banish all traces...
We can push all large items away from the walls,
And over here's where you can keep all your tools.

Whatever you want, you can have straight away –
I think I might just keep you busy all day!
The secret, I've heard, to great decoration,
Is to not rush the stage that we call 'preparation'...

A clean and smooth surface is really essential,
If the finish will fulfil the painter's potential.
For some stubborn patches, you might need a heat gun,
I think you're pleased to see me, or you've already got one!

Now, I'll hold your ladder, while you get it up,

Its extendable length is a bit of good luck…

Let me hand you your scraper and watch you get stripping,

Rub hard at these bumps, oops, my masking tape's slipping!


So throw down a dust sheet to catch what you splash,

Was that synthetic bristle, or just your moustache?

Come on, unhinge my doors, they're ready for dipping;

I like a gloss finish, but not all that dripping.


Hurry!  Size me up, price me up, give me a quote -

Your Dulux is in, you've 'pooled' - now grab your one-coat!


******

*Some like it hot!*

# Ode to a Charismatic Coalman

When the flames have died down and my embers need
stirring,

It could be a shortage of fuel is occurring.

If I've plenty of paper and no lack of kindling,

It must be my store of the hard stuff that's dwindling.

I'll call you out, Coal Man, and with any luck,

You'll be up like a shot in your big, flat-bed truck.

You know how important you are for my heating,

(And, furthermore, that you'll receive a warm greeting).

The size of your load is quite awe-inspiring,

You've got what I need to keep a big fire in;

Some crackle and fizz and my chimney is smoking,

My up draught is strong, but I'll still need some poking.

Now, some coal men's coal simply can't make the grade,

But your coal is so good, you deserve to be paid.

So show me your invoice, I don't mind a few smudges…

I can get a bit dirty without bearing grudges.

Look! I've swept out my hearth in anticipation

Of your out of sight, anthracite, burning sensation.

If your coal's a bit damp, and heating up slow,

I'll kneel down with my bellows and have a quick blow.

And let's not forget, if you're into tradition,

To welcome the New Year, the old superstition

That, in crossing one's threshold, a coal man brings luck,

Well, I'm lucky already, so just give me a…bag of coal!

******

*Hook, line and sinker…*

# Ode to a Fishy-Fingered Fisherman

For a dishy man, a fisherman can hardly be bettered,

Be he oil-skinned, wadered or thick woolly sweatered.

I know, 'cos I'm surfing those websites 'til dawn –

Am I getting addicted to internet prawn?

If you show me your flies, then I'll get your hook ready,

Gaze into my eyes while I hold your rod steady.

I'll learn all you can teach about mackerel and skate,

And you can look on as I master bait…

As pungent and salty as anchovy paste,

Your fisherman's friend has a rather odd taste.

If my riverbed's dry and things get a bit humdrum,

I've heard fish oil's good for an omega threesome.

So come, view my aquarium, fill up my tank,

And think only of me when you're having a

Wakeful moment.

******

*Behold! A magnificent cock!*

# Ode to a Frisky Farmer

A farmer's your man if you want a full day,

His cock's crowing at dawn when he's up to make hay.

He doesn't need sleep when he hears nature's calls,

He's the man, so I've heard, and I know he's got bulls.

A hit in his field, a farm-yard go-getter,

A wow in the saddle, (but bare back much better),

Ploughs a very deep furrow, getting down in my field,

If he handles these udders, he'll increase my yield.

He's chemical-free, so there's no need to panic,

His produce is yummy, yes, he's multi-organic.

He knows cattle and sheep, pig, goat, chicken and duck,

He's a big, friendly farmer, and a bloody great…

Farmer.

\*\*\*

*Oops!*

# Ode to a Frolicsome Firefighter

I wake late at night – is that smoke I can smell?

All alone in the dark, it can be hard to tell…

999 operator says, "Which service, please?"

With anticipation, I'm weak at the knees:

"Firemen please, and not just one or two,

My fire's so hot that I need a whole crew!"

Yes, I'm all hot and bothered, flames licking my thatches,

(I've been a bad girl, I've been playing with matches!)

The sound of the sirens is so reassuring,

(Nights in on your own can get pretty boring) …

Quick, get out your ladder – I'm on the top floor.

Should I hang out the window, or press up to the door?

If that gets jammed shut, you'll need cutting equipment,

So, bring your big chopper – (no Freudian slip meant).

Once you're in and the door's from its hinges adrift,

You can bring me down safe with a fireman's lift.

Now, a fireman's lift is a move of precision,

And over the shoulder's a novel position.

If that's what it takes to see a real man,

Be assured, you're adored! I've no hosepipe ban!

See? I've got what it takes to keep firemen coming:

Electrical hazard, inadequate plumbing…

So come on, aim your hose at the base of my fire,

Your towering inferno just got a bit higher!

My pussy needs rescuing – climb into my tree,

Oops, I'm trapped in this clothing, so quick – cut me free!

I'll drive into a pond, jam my toe in a tap,

With that uniform on, you're my kind of chap…

Know that MEN from the BOYS may thus be distinguished:

By the size of the wet patch when my fire's extinguished!

******

*Bang Bang!*

# Ode to a Luverly Lawyer

In matters libidinous, I'll make my case,

For a man who's much more than a handsome face;

There's something luscious in a lawyer, whoever he be,

The dirty devil's in the detail, LLB.

I need a brief encounter, so don't take offence,

If I ask to watch you mounting a robust defence.

I could do it myself, with the cost just a fraction,

But you've more grounds of appeal than a straight civil action.

We can retire to your chambers if you're called to the bar,

With a caseload like that, you're bound to go far.

I'll submit to cross-examination.

When your Crown court's next in session,

With some nifty litigation

I'll be nine-tenths in your possession.

So, court me with your codicil, advance me your directive,

If I'm intestate just sort me out a spell inside (corrective)!

So, place your right hand here and swear an oath

To God, the Law and Duty;

All rise!  I know I'm going down,

And that, m'Lud's, a beauty!!

*Tight nuts?*

# Ode to a Mucho Macho Mechanic

When my starting handle needs a crank,

And my engine isn't stirring,

There's no tiger roaring in my tank,

Just a pussy who's not purring –

I need some help, a man who can,

A mechanic on the job,

To restore to health my clutch control

And make my engine throb.

You might hear a screech when I'm coming,

'Cos this fanbelt's just no good –

So go round the front and bend over,

I'll pull the knob and pop my hood…

Check my levels, check my pressures,

Before, behind and below,

And if that doesn't get things moving,

Use this rope, tie it on and tow

Me to your inspection pit

And check out my fine undercarriage;

If there's nothing quicker than a Kwik Fit fitter,

I'll want extra time in your garage!

So come on, oil my gear box,

And test my emissions,

I give peak performance

In the wettest conditions.

I need filling up –

Hold your nozzle, start pumping;

My battery's flat,

Here's a lead – let's get jumping!

0-60 in seconds – a personal best,

Now let's get in the car,

And put that to the test!


******

*Full swivel action!*

# Ode to a Debonair Dentist

It generally happens just two times a year,

And I get quite excited when I see the time's near,

For my oral needs are fundamental,

So I relish all my check-ups (dental)…

And if, in between, I feel a slight ache,

I know who to call, and no mistake;

For an ache turns to throb in the wink of an eye,

If you can relieve it, you're my kind of guy!

Now, let me lie down in your easy-clean chair,

Switch on your big lamp –

Turn it up to full glare.

Just say the word and I'll open wide,

Are those latex gloves?  Get your fingers inside!

Explain the procedure – I'm fully consentin',

Treat hard parts and soft parts, enamel and dentin.

As you get busy, my mouth is so full,

And delaying a swallow is making me drool…

That can get messy, but won't be an issue,

When I have at the ready, an absorbent tissue.

A packet in one's pocket means worrying less

About leakage and spillage and making a mess.

You can get them singly, but like most girls I know,

I get multiple ones, when I'm on the go –

I love to feel a full packet and, for any guy,

A pre-opened box is most welcome nearby.

During this appointment, you'll be only mine,

And my mouth's your chance to really shine.

The sight of your equipment gives me a strange feeling,

So I'll lay back a while and gaze at your ceiling.

You can tell your assistant you want to start drilling,

You can see I've a hole that is desperate for filling;

She can help with some suction, so give her a shout-

So your drill's good and ready, she can get her bits out.

You make a great team, and, as you can see,

I'm very relaxed as you both work on me.

The mask's a nice touch – you gaze over the top,

And we all know the signal if I need you to stop.

Once you've finished with me, my lips feel quite numb,

Guess they'll look a bit puffy for some time to come…

Yes, my dentist makes smiles and never a pout,

I'll just have a quick rinse and then spit this stuff out (!)

******

*It's all hard wood!*

# Ode to an Upstanding Undertaker

You might think I'm just having a lie-in,

But truth be told, I'm thinking of dyin'.

I grave your attention, so make no mistake, a

Girl will do what she must, to get her undertaker.


You're the man of the moment if the moment's heart-stopping,

So come a bit closer, see my vital signs dropping.

It's no do-gooding doctor this body's requiring,

You're on a dead cert, it's X-rated, I'm X-piring.


In a hushed, husky whisper, let's talk about us,

And the finer points of my sarcophagus…

For my casket I think I'll have satin-lined oak,

A soft, pink, silky lining's what I want when I croak.


I don't mind if you're Protestant, Catholic or Druid,

Just as long as you're generous with your embalming fluid.

You're drop dead gorgeous in your dark funeral suit,

In the hearse, pimp my ride with a floral tribute.

I'll do what it takes to get six feet under,

I *want* to be the victim of a medical blunder!

As my life ebbs away, my inhibitions decreasing,

Hey! The latest style is necrophile and I'm deceasing!


Fling off my mortal coil and bury this stiffy,

Get me deep down and dirty before I get niffy…

You might think this bad taste but some things are much sicker –

Three in one?  A dog collar? Well, hello…

More tea, Vicar?


******

Printed in Great Britain
by Amazon

34898711R00034